Up, Up, Up

by Asa Spahn   illustrated Roberta Collier-Morales

Orlando   Boston   Dallas   Chicago   San Diego

Visit *The Learning Site!*

www.harcourtschool.com

Copyright © by Harcourt, Inc.

All rights reserved. No part of this publication may be reproduced or transmitted in any form or by any means, electronic or mechanical, including photocopy, recording, or any information storage and retrieval system, without permission in writing from the publisher.

Requests for permission to make copies of any part of the work should be addressed to School Permissions and Copyrights, Harcourt, Inc., 6277 Sea Harbor Drive, Orlando, Florida 32887-6777. Fax: 407-345-2418.

HARCOURT and the Harcourt Logo are trademarks of Harcourt, Inc., registered in the United States of America and/or other jurisdictions.

Printed in China

ISBN 0-15-325434-3

14 15 16 17 18 19 20 985 10 09 08 07 06

Ordering Options
ISBN 0-15-323766-X (Collection)
ISBN 0-15-329606-2 (package of 5)

I go up, up, up.
What do I see?

I see a red fox run.
Look at it run, run, run.

I see a little bird tap.
Look at it tap, tap, tap.

I see a big deer sip.
Look at it sip, sip, sip.

I see a tan rabbit hop.
Look at it hop, hop, hop.

I see a fat cub nap.
Look at it nap, nap, nap.

I am at the top.
I see a big sun set.
Look at it set, set, set.